# MORE POEMS
# TO
# GALORE

# MORE POEMS
## TO
# GALORE

GERALD G. MOOTHART

**ARPress**
ILLUMINATING IDEAS.
EMPOWERING VOICES

**ARPress**
45 Dan Road Suite 5
Canton MA 02021

Hotline: 1(888) 821-0229
Fax:     1(508) 545-7580


Ordering Information:
Quantity sales. Special discounts are available on quantity purchases by corporations, associations, and others. For details, contact the publisher at the address above.


Printed in the United States of America.


ISBN-13:  Softcover        979-8-89356-465-5
          eBook            979-8-89356-464-8

Library of Congress Control Number: 2024904601

# Table of Contents

# "THEY CALL ME THE GRAND OLD FLAG"

When I was first made from silk and thread,
and what I stand for as they all said.
It made me want to fly and see,
The Great Respect they gave to me.
When I was raised on the pole so high,
To wave in the breeze as the people go by.
They stood at attention as I was raised,
once on high they'd stand to gaze.
Lives were given in protection of me,
in wars on land and battles at sea.
But things have changed as time went by,
People don't care and I don't know why.
I have done nothing that I can see,
for them to lose their respect for me.
I'll try to tell you what hurts me most,
as I fly so proudly on my post.
When it comes time to take me down,
they know I'm not to touch the ground.
But they don't care what they drag me through,
and they don't care what they have to do.
Instead of being folded in the proper way,
they roll me in a ball like an armful of hay.
Taken inside to be stowed for the night,
in the closet or drawer just out of sight.
Some don't even bother to take me downa
they leave me up the whole year round.
They don't remember I need a light on me,
so at night the world will know and see.
How proud I am as I fly at night,
as I fly and wave in the beautiful light.
As I Wave to those who should pass me by,
they don't bother to look and I don't know why.
But it makes me sad as I wave on high,

some people don't even take time to try.
To understand what I stand for then,
stand for now, and way back when.
So here I am as I am told,
folded up or even unrolled.
I'll wave up here and I won't sag,
and I'll still be known as your Grand Old Flag.

# "OUR NATIONAL BIRD"

An Eagle soars in Heavenly skies,
and floats upon a breeze.
With oh such care from way up there,
and does it with such ease.

So graceful as it glides along,
to climb and dip for speed.
A mother bird in search for pray,
her young for her to feed.

As she glides her merry way,
her eyes upon the ground.
She climbs and dips so beautifully,
until that pray is found.

Into a dive from where she is,
with target kept in sight.
She clamps her claws around that pray,
while she is still in flight.

Then off to feed the little ones,
wherever they may be.
High upon some mountain cliff,
away from you and me.

It's no wonder now my friend,
of all the tales you've heard.
That we should pick this beautiful foul,
to be our National Bird.

# "THE FLIGHT OF OUR BIRD"

No words can express from what I've heard,
The beauty and keenness of our national bird.
As seen, flying today in the skies above,
creating a picture that we all love.

To just stand there today, with that bird in view,
there's nothing more exciting for us to do.
keeping that bird within our sight,
and watching it perform, there in it's flight.

That bird is out there as we all know,
gliding and dipping to and fro.
up and down, and in and out,
showing to us what it's all about.

I thank all those in times long ago,
the ones that had to really know.
agreed from all of what they had heard,
and picked this foul to be our national bird.

## "KEEP AMERICA FREE"

Never a story has been told,
in the past to young and old.
But I'll tell you one, just listen to me,
that Grand Old Flag is something to see.

High on the pole up in the air,
makes you stop and want to stare.
The more you look and don't realize,
that Grand Old Flag can hypnotize.

It's beauty in it's breath taking way,
will always make you want to say.
The Pledge of Allegiance to our old glory,
and that alone would make a story.

It waves to you from upon high,
a beautiful sight it's make you cry.
To stop and think whenever you see,
about living in a country that is always free.

So where ever you go, whatever you do,
always keep the past so true.
Teach to all what has to be,
and work to KEEP AMERICA FREE.

# "FLY THE AMERICAN FLAG"

To live in a country, the greatest on earth,
and to share it's liberty, for what it's worth.
We should be thankful, yes every one,
for what's given to us, as it was done.

Liberty is not free for you or for me,
it never has been and never will be.
Many lives were lost in days of our past,
forming our country in the mold they cast.

Now it's our job, keeping liberty so true,
sharing our lives in whatever we do.
polishing our country all of the time,
always keeping liberty on our mind.

As true Americans, as we say we are,
playing our parts, and becoming a star.
as God picked this country to be our home,
let's show our thanks wherever we roam.

Showing our colors, the RED, WHITE and BLUE
these colors to us that are so true.
In days ahead, from morning till night,
fly the American Flag, and fly it right.

# "THE STARS AND STRIPES"

The stars and strips of our "OLD GLORY",
within this poem shall tell the story.
Continental Congress chose red, white and blue,
as our national colors so beautiful and true.
It represents our country as everyone feels,
its people, our government and our national ideals.
For many years it has stood, for our liberty,
justice, and democracy for you and for me.
Hundreds of millions of people have lived in the past,
under the flag of our country and the trails that it cast.
Millions have fought and died for our liberty,
while building America, the land of the free.
Seven red and six white stripes, with a union of blue,
along with thirteen white stars, in a circle so true.
Was the first flag of our country, resolved in 1777,
number of flags today, brings the total to twenty-seven.
As the years went by and other states joined the union,
more stars were added to the flag for their communion.
Nine rows of stars, there on the union to be seen,
representing our fifty states so neat and so keen.
Honor and respect each day, this flag we so love,
its beauty on the pole as it waves from above.
Stand at attention and salute it, as it passes by,
in folding an unfolding and we all know why.
Be proud you live in America, the land of the free,
displaying the colors of our country for all to see.

# "IN UNITED AS WE ALL STAND"

A tragedy hit the other day, and took us by surprise.
It did not bothered everyone, but sure did open eyes.
For those victims of the hit, there's not much we can do.
For all the loved ones left behind, our prayers go out to you.

The tragedy the terrorist cause, throughout the world each day
We all have read and thought about, but not much we could say,
But sooner or later, down the road, it did come home it's true.
Within our future that lies ahead, We'll pick what's best to do.

The thought that bothers me today, is why we never thought.
To think the problems over there, to our country could not be brought.
We worked so hard in days gone by, to help those countries out.
Sooner or later we should have known, they'd come to retaliate their pout.

Those that govern this country today, right from the very top,
and those from other countries too, should work to make it stop.
The Terrorists that cause all this pain, no matter where it's true.
Should be made, to pay the price, for the hardships that they do.

Let's all join hands, as one in hope, and work to do our part,
strive to retain that liberty, we hold so dear to our heart.
Donate blood, support the fund, and be generous to a plus.
Our freedom of liberty is at stake, and it depends on us.

Think of your ancestors in days gone by, and what they did for you.
In building this country we live in today, it's foundation is so true.
Freedom you'll find is never free, yes, take your part in hand.
and join the others as a group, "In United As We All Stand."

# "MAKE IT A SLOWER TIME TODAY"

As one wakes each morning,
and opens up their eyes.
they see the bright sun shining,
to them it's no surprise.

They leave the bed behind them,
to start a brand-new day.
The format of the program,
for each in their own way.

As you progress forward,
while problems come in view.
You overcome these hardships,
to the best as you can do

For when the day is over,
as time it goes by fast.
you'll think about the future,
and less about the past.

You'll keep within your memories,
of what you did today.
and say a prayer to God above,
for his guidance in his own way.

The paths our lives are leading,
zooming by if I must say,
Gear down, let up on the petal
"MAKE IT A SLOWER TIME TODAY".

# "ONE DAY AT A TIME"

As we all try to meditate,
down life's merry road.
struggling with all our hardships,
and lugging our heavy load.

Awake to face each tomorrow,
a first step to really shine,
and keep within our memories,
to take one day at a time.

With caring and sharing among us,
while honesty is there it's true.
Being loyal to those around us,
is what we strive to do.

Each life's a one-way venture,
make changes as you go,
for there's no instant replay,
from the results of the seeds we sow.

# "A WISH FOR YOU"

Today's a day I wish for you, ordinary miracles you will find,
they all will fit within your day, makes a life for you so kind.
A pot of coffee you didn't have to make, fills eyes with many tears,
An unexpected phone call from a friend, you haven't seen in years.

Green stoplights on your way to work, or if your out to shop,
I wish for you a day of little things, where you can reap your crop.
The fastest lines your standing in, so you don't have to wait,
A good sing along song on the radio, and these you'll never hate.

Your keys right where you look for them, cause they are hard to
find,
The weatherman to bless you always, with great weather as he is
kind.
I wish a day of happiness and little bite-size pieces of perfec-
tion, that give you the funny feeling. that the Lord's smiling with
his protection.

He's holding you so gently, because you are a someone special and
rare,
I wish you a day of Peace, Happiness and Joy, while under his
special care.
They say it takes a minute to find that special person, and always
this is met, an hour to appreciate them, a day to love them, and a
life time to forget.

Give this poem to all the people that you promise you will never
forget,
and let them know of your promises, these rules that you have set.
Enjoy your life in the future, remembering friends in what you do,
Remember this poem that you have given, that's named "A WISH
FOR YOU".

# "IN THE YEAR OF NINETEEN O THREE"

The year is 1903, one hundred years ago,
a different century then and most don't really know.
Here are the US statistics, in that year of nineteen o three,
compare it to the present time, boggles minds, for it did me.

The average life expectancy in the US was forty-seven,
half the life today for some, when they are called to heaven.
Only 14 percent of homes, had a bathtub for their care,
washed their bodies once a week, time they couldn't spare

Only 8 percent of homes, had a telephone for their use,
not like for us today my friend, this item we put to abuse.
Three minutes calls from Denver, to New York then to make,
cost eleven dollars my friend, in this conversation to partake.

There were only 8,000 cars, in the US a big king size toy,
and 144 miles of paved roads, on Sunday drives to enjoy.
Maximum speed limit in most cities, was 10 miles per hour,
how many tickets were passed out, for the people to devour?

The average US worker made between $200 and $400 per year,
after expenses in their life at that time, running out was never a
fear.
A competent accountant could expect to earn, $2000 in their pay,
yes, a dentist $2500 per year, to cover expenses in every way.

More than 95 percent of all births, in the US took place at home,
to hospitals today a few don't make it, in their travels as they roam.
Sugar cost four cents a pound, and eggs were 14 cents a dozen,
priced today at these costs, we'd think that we were a buzzing.

Coffee cost fifteen cents a pound, and most enjoyed each sip,
at the cost of coffee today, that price wouldn't cover the tip.
Most women only washed their hair, once a month at that time,
used borax or egg yolks for shampoo, to make it look just fine.

The five leading causes of death, in the US were at that time,
Pneumonia, influenza and tuberculosis, three that were prime.
Heart disease and stroke two more, yes to complete the list,
in the deaths as today, for each person they were all mist.

The American flag had 45 stars, for them to enjoy at that time,
three states, Hawaii and Alaska, fill the pattern of today's design.
The population of Las Vegas, in Nevada 30 was on the list,
canned beer, iced tea hadn't been invented, today they would be
missed.

There were no Mother's or Father's day, great times of our days,
one in ten US adults couldn't read or write, to cover all their ways.
Only six percent of Americans had graduated from high school,
they didn't take the precious time, to learn that golden rule.

Marijuana, heroin and morphine, over the counter you could buy,
at the corner drugstores, no matter wherever you would try.
According to one pharmacist, heroin clears the complexion,
and gives buoyancy to the mind, and both with perfection.

Eighteen percent of households had a full-time servant or maid,
there is no way to figure this, built into today's modern trade.
There were only about 250 reported murders, in the entire USA,
compare that final figure, in the reports that are turned in today.

If we look back at the progress, our world has made in 100 years,
down the road we could have problems, these could cause some
tears.
This progress brings us livelihood, it covers cost that we all enjoy,
But in the future we must be careful, this world it could destroy.

# "ALL THE WAY"

Life is unpredictable,
as you live each day by day.
You pick and choose your commitments,
while each one comes your way.

As you smooth out all the sadness,
the happiness you'll enjoy.
You'll find as you go on living,
that your life is not a toy.

He put you here for a reason,
his reason you'll never know.
For when you've fulfilled his purpose,
back to heaven he'll see that you go.

As you travel this one way venture,
do the best in your life each day,
Be thankful he choose you from his roster,
he has faith in you all the way.

# "A CHRISTMAS WISH TO A FRIEND"

A card is not enough for you,
a friend so dear and just as true.
My blessings come to you in this way,
wishing for you a special day.

May Christmas be the best you've had,
full of happiness and nothing sad.
May Santa fill your wishes in his way,
with ever thing that fits within his sleigh.

Feed those rein deer with plenty of food,
treat them gentle and don't be rude.
We need them to come East on Xmas eve,
so Santa can eat all the food we leave.

Share the day with your family,
with all of them and the friends you see.
Don't eat too much of the food put out,
for it will make you more that stout.

My best to you for a great New Year,
filled with happiness and lots of cheer.
Enjoy each day as they come your way,
for you, what more can I really say.

I'll close this blessing with many sweet words,
most of them you've already heard.
take care of yourself, enjoy your family,
best enjoyments of your life you'll ever see.

# "OBSERVATION IS A GAME"

Observation is a game,
that everyone should play.
There is no end to what you'll learn,
within your given day.

The drivers as they drive their car,
the rules that they all break.
The speed they drive so carelessly,
the short cuts they all take.

Now people are the best choice,
for they are number one.
When it comes down to observing,
here's where you have the fun.

The different types of clothes they wear,
and how they stand and walk,
the expressions of their hand and face,
each time they try to talk.

How they all act in public,
especially in a crowd.
Most aren't worth being near,
because they talk too loud.

I've learned a many a lesson,
from observing in every way,
and I'll keep right on observing,
until my dying day.

# "A SENSE OF A GOOSE"

When you see the geese a flying,
in the formation of a V.
This to us is really beautiful,
and something nice to see.

You might consider science,
has discovered as to why,
these beautiful birds in their travel,
have picked this way to fly.

As each bird flops its wings,
in doing so it creates an uplift,
for the bird immediately following,
in a path that is not so swift.

By flying in V formation,
the whole flock adds a greater length.
In the distance they have flown,
and still keep up with their strength.

Geese who share a common direction,
and sense of community can get,
to where they are going more quickly,
without the fear and sweat.

Because they all are traveling,
on the trust of one another,
and this to me makes more sense,
as they are Sister and Brother.

When a goose falls out of formation,
it suddenly feels the drag.
It quickly gets back into formation,

where it can pick up the sag.
If we have as much sense as a goose,
we will all stay in formation,
with those people who are headed,
and working in the same direction.

When the head goose, it gets tired,
it rotates back in the wing,
and another goose flies the point,
so it can hear the others sing.

It is sensible to take turns,
while doing demanding jobs,
whether your with people,
or with this flying mob.

Geese honk from behind to encourage,
those up front to keep their speed.
What messages do we give,
when we honk from behind as we lead.
Finally and this is important,
when a goose gets sick or is shot,
and falls out of formation,
no longer to fill his spot.

Two other geese fall out with the disable,
and follow it to help in their tries.
They stay with the fallen goose,
till it's able to fly or it dies.

Only then do they launch out on their own,
or with another formation,
to catch up with their group,
and to continue to their destination.
 If we have the sense of a goose,
we will stand by each other like that.
We'll work as a team for our Fraternity,
as we work to improve it's format.

I ask you to take a good look,
as to the condition of our Order at hand.
to join hands as a team in working,
and to make this a more freedom land.

## "TOUCHED BY AN ANGEL"

Touched by an Angel, with that gentle touch,
to each of us, should mean so much.
While in our lives, take time to care,
and thank the Lord, we have love to share.

Our blessing to those, within our reach,
should be our goals, to always teach.
To live our lives, as days come and go,
and thank the Lord, for this row we hoe.

We are on this earth, for only his reason,
to do a job, throughout each season.
we're all under his care, for this is true,
he'll recall our name, when our job is through,

So when you rise, on each given day,
praise his grace, in some small way.
Be most thankful to him, for his gift of love,
and carry out your job, till your called above.

# "A BUTTERFLY"

A pretty butterfly is gorgeous to see,
so beautiful in the eyes of the.
Just to watch each dip and swoop,
free to venture outside it's coop.

As it flies on it's merry way.
looking for food each sunny day.
Keeping an eye on those in sight,
as it continues it's outstanding flight.

Both up and down and in and out,
so flexible, so limber and stout.
each flower becomes a stepping stone,
there perched so beautiful on it's throne.

Field trips taken by children from school,
for them to learn their golden rule.
Observe these creatures, one and all,
beginning in spring summer and fall.

What they see, they will enjoy,
as outstanding to them as any old toy.
You too could learn, if you wanted to,
for this beautiful sight is there to view.

# "FOR HIS GUIDANCE AND FOR HIS CARES"

While among all those at present,
join together where you may go.
help contribute to all the happiness,
and the satisfaction to make it so.

As you travel down the highways,
and the by-ways of our land.
Let us all be very thankful,
our blessed Father holds our hand.

Along with him, our guiding angle
keeps us constant in her view,
Always there to help protect us,
in every thing that we may do.

For once upon the highways,
among those that are around.
Your safety in your traveling,
to me, really isn't, that sound.

For all the crazy drivers,
out there upon each road.
The speeding and the swaying,
I'm sure will dump their load.

I'm hoping and I'm praying,
for each and every one.
While you are in your travels,
you are protected while having fun.

During at all times, be a believer,
and don't hesitate to say your prayers.
Thank the Good Lord for his protection,
for his guidance and for his cares.

# WHAT IS FRIENDSHIP?

Friendship is a blessing,
We work to generate.
The hardships we encounter,
in trying to create.

The love of one another,
the trust that we impound.
The bond between two people,
that makes a friendship sound.

# "FOUR SEASONS IN NEW ENGLAND"

It's Spring time in New England, enjoy each day with care,
The buds are popping all over, here and everywhere.
The smell of all the flowers, a scent you can enjoy,
The beauty of those colors, more precious than a toy.

The gorgeous days of summer, for they will come and go,
And live them to there fullest, to you make them just so.
Enjoy the beach for swimming, or camping if you like,
Or hiking in the mountains, while riding your trail bike.

Autumn comes our way, the leaves now covered with dew
The beauty of the horizon, the leaf peeker's come to view.
Those pictures that are taken, a corner stone for our past,
The history while we are living, a reminder as we cast.

Now winter is a coming, we're guarantied of that,
Put away your famous baseball, along with your bat.
Bundle up more comfy, as temperature they descend,
Wear your clothes in layers, for this is the trend.

With snow on the ground and flurries in the air,
One should, when you are walking, do it with such care.
It could be very icy, beneath that beautiful snow,
and if your not very careful, down I'm sure you'll go.

Now take it from a person, yes one of seventy two,
The four seasons of New England are great for me and you.
The flowers in the spring time, the beauty of each fall,
Warm temperatures in the summer, so one can play baseball.

Christmas wouldn't be Christmas, unless snow is on the ground,
It takes snow covering everything, for Santa to get around.
Plan to visit New England, before it becomes too late,
A season of New England, and put aside that special date

# "A SMOKERS PRAYER"

OUR HEAVENLY FATHER,
hear my prayer,
I ask of you my life to spare.
Each day I know I should behave,
and stay away from things I crave,
The cigarettes I long to smoke,
somehow they really make me choke.
The pleasures in the past, I've had,
today somehow I know is bad.
So in your guidance from above,
help me stop these things I love.
Help me with my life to save,
and keep me from these things I crave.
Help me in these times of wonder,
if you don't I'll be six feet under.
"AMEN"

# "OUR REQUEST TO A FRIEND"

I tell you smokers it's no joke,
of all the cigarettes that you may smoke.
You get that urge, you reach for the pack,
if it wasn't there you'd be on track.

On track to change to something new,
to quit that smoking that you now do.
to bring your life into your hand,
and show the world you have command.

Each time you light and puff away,
say to yourself in some small way.
you know it's wrong in what you do,
it's bad for your health and this is true.

So from now on I'll replace that pack,
with gum, to chew, or a small snack.
A toothpick, placed between my lips,
the hand would pick up in it's trips.

For once a few days have gone by,
with these changes that you may try.
will be the best in your life it's true,
only suggested for you to do.

You've seen the changes within the past,
the cost increase has gone up fast.
The rules have changed as to where you smoke,
some of these places it's really no joke.

The world is watching in what you do,
the choice, we know, is up to you.
As friends, we look, we hope, we pray,
you'll give up smoking on a future day.

## "A MOTHER'S LOVE"

A Mother's love I never had,
She died, when I was just a lad.
She filled her job, at age twenty-four,
God called her to heaven to do no more.
My love for her is always there,
if she had lived, I know she'd care.
I've wondered how her love would be,
living today, so I could see.
Doing for her in a special way,
and hugging her each "Mother's Day".

# "MOHAWK TRAIL"

The big trail was the pathway,
the five nations Indian tread.
As they crossed the Berkshire Mountains,
down the winding cold riverbed.

Thirty-eight miles of winding rivers,
is what they used to come through.
To make their way to New England,
to help the settlers as they grew.

Following the Cold and Deerfield Rivers,
as they ran down hills to the East.
The Indians used this pathway,
in search for food for feast.

As time went on a wagon road,
followed portions of the old foot trail.
And today a super highway, Route 2,
to bring us food, tourist and mail.

An eight-foot bronze Indian Statue,
a nine ton boulder stands.
Looking way out towards the East world,
and up without stretched hands.

This Memorial to the Mohawk Indians,
looking across the Deerfield River at its site,
is something for everyone to see,
either in the morning, noon or night.


You may travel where the road may take you,
or where ever your boat may sail,
but you have not seen America, my friend,
till you have viewed the Mohawk Trail.

# "FRATERNITY"

F. is for the fellowship among us,
R. is for the rules for our guide,
A. is for the attendance that we show it,
T. is for the time we put aside,
E. is for the effort in our trying,
R. is for our ritualistic looks,
N. is for the nice things in our programs,
I. is for the idea's in our books,
T. is for the trust we build within us,
Y. is for the youth we need to grow,
Put them all together they spell FRATERNITY,
the seeds for our success that we must sow.

# "LEAVES GALORE"

Somehow we need to find a way,
in which our leaves will create some pay.
We have so many this time of date,
is there something we can create.

They are so nice to see in the spring
the birds among them as they all sing,
larger on into summer as they all grow,
to increase their beauty as we all know.

Then into fall as the coldness begins,
their colors change and here is our wins.
The leaf peek's come from everywhere,
to see all the colors under Gods care.

But this doesn't help when leaves they fall,
blown by the winds into mountains or a wall.
Covering the ground as far as you can see,
but not out of sight of either you or of me.

There should be a use, if we all think hard,
to use these leaves raked up from our yard,
As insulation in winter, a bedding for our cows,
also for little piglets along with all other sows.

When shredded as a compose, dried to it's best,
for packing when shipping would be a great test.
Covering your garden to keep weeds from growing,
to take away the hard job of all of the hoeing.

I'm sure if we thought hard we'd come up with a way,
to find a good produce to ourselves it would pay,
In all things we recycle it too could be done
turn leaves into a product that would be number one.

# "HAPPY BIRTHDAY BROTHER"

As I set with pen in hand,
about to write to you.
I reminisce of days gone by,
and things we use to do.

But that was many years ago,
still seems like yesterday.
Good times we had when we were kids,
the games we use to play.

But time goes by so very fast,
as days they come and go,
and you will never realize,
just how we love you so.

Another day has come for you,
and we are proud to say.
Happy Birthday Brother dear,
may it be a special day

# "LONG STEM YELLOW ROSES"

Roses are so pretty,
when they are in full bloom.
The fragment of their essence,
when picked you will consume.

They grow in many colors,
for all of us to see.
I only buy the yellow ones,
my wife will sure agree.

It gives me oh such pleasure,
to see the look upon her face.
When she spots two dozen yellow ones,
so nicely in a vase.

It hurts me oh so deeply,
for when I have to buy.
Two dozen yellow long stems,
I almost have to cry.

For in my heart their gorgeous,
to look at and to smell.
For I know they die quickly,
no matter if kept well.

So in their place I purchase,
Carnations long and true.
A flower just as pretty,
and last a week or two.

# "JUST ME AND YOU"

As I stand here on the footstep,
and the doorway to your heart.
I will plan our lives as one dear,
and hope that we won't part.

But you can never tell these days,
what fate may have in store.
For I may stop loving you,
if you become a bore.

Still, that was many years ago,
as you can plainly see.
For when we picked each other dear,
I guess it was meant to be.

I'll work to keep you happy,
in everything that you do.
As long as you will promise me,
it will only be me and you.

# "A FIRE EXTINGUISHER FOR YOUR USE"

Fire extinguishers are your small fire defense,
and should be used with common sense.
learn your extinguisher from A to Z,
use your knowledge and you will see.

Many things you learn will come to view,
and in the end will be helpful to you.
'The rights, the wrongs, the ins and out,
with the proper facts there will be no doubt.

Your fire extinguisher of your desire,
must be the one to fight the fire.
One to fit A, B, or C,
use the proper one, maybe all three.

Remember the word PASS, when it's time for you,
to fight the fire in what you do.
Pull the pin and Aim it low,
Squeeze the handle and let it go.

A Sweeping motion from side to side,
when you do all this, the fire can't hide.
Once it's out still be alert,
if it flames again, give it a squirt.

Before you attempt, the fire to fight,
see the people have left, the building right.
Make sure the fire department is on it's way,
then you should decide if it will pay.

If the fire is spreading don't be insane,
if the operation of the extinguishers your untrained,
if at all there may be of any doubt,
then leave it to the firemen to put it out.

## "SORRY TIMES ON THANKSGIVING"

On this day at Thanksgiving time,
we have much to be thankful for.
Thankful that we have our health,
and really for many things more.

Sorry we can't be with you,
to share in all your prayers.
But knowing that we're remembered,
is all that really cares.

## "A CHRISTMAS GREETING"

Merry Christmas to one and all,
Good Luck to you and have a ball.
Our thoughts are always there with you,
We hope that yours are with us too.
May God protect each and every one,
throughout the day as you have fun.
Take time within this blessed day,
to thank the Lord in a special way.

# "POUNDS, POUNDS AND POUNDS"

Food, food, anything sweet,
Oh how I just love to eat.
When I shop in a grocery store,
I only buy what I adore.

This is bad as you can see,
there is twice as much of me.
I'm as round as I am tall,
guess I'll have to get on the ball.

Where do you go, what do you do?
to take the pounds back off of you.
I'm ashamed when I go out,
I just stay home so I can pout.

is a sickness like all the rest,
I try to cut down, I do my best.
But I'm addicted to food you know,
and all it does is make me grow.

I go to bed and hope and pray,
I pray the pounds will go away.
Maybe someday God will be good to me,
and I'll be thin, you wait and see.

# "HER CHRISTMAS WILL BE WHITE"

I gazed upon a Christmas tree,
back in my home city.
It was on the village green,
and my was it so pretty.

The lights were shinning all around,
all colors that were bright.
With snow upon the branches too,
to complete that pretty sight.

As I gazed upon this tree,
that kept me hypnotized.
I saw this girl standing there,
and she was sure surprised.

I guess that she had never seen,
a tree like this before.
From birth she had been blinded,
and her sight was just restored.

From this I know the feeling,
a miracle that is right,
and she will be so thankful,
that her Christmas will be white.

# "BE THANKFUL YOUR JOB IS DONE"

I know that you are down and out,
and you think that life's unfair.
But for this very thought my friend,
he knows that you will care.

He put you here into this world,
with a special job to do.
He knows that you will do the job,
and work till you are through.

Some jobs are small and take less time,
if this is in your case.
Then you should be very pleased my friend,
he trusts that you can face.

He never closes a door on you,
without opening another one.
Be thankful that your job is through,
and think of the up coming fun.

While others live a longer life,
and suffer all the way.
I know that they would be so glade,
to take your place today.

# "COOK YOUR FOOD AT HOME"

With all the fast food outlets,
we have in this world today.
One would never think to cook,
at home in any way.
The mess that is avoided,
the time you have to spare.
Many people love it,
others don't really care.
But let's take a better look,
at what you don't like to do.
Cooking really isn't that bad,
it's fun for me and you.
Tie pies, the cakes and cookies,
the salads that you arrange,
I'm sure when you get started,
You'll find that it's not strange.
Some people are more gifted,
than others in this chore.
Some think that it's exciting,
others think that it's a bore.
Now let's think of commercial cooking,
and all the things you buy.
For when you read the labels,
you'll really want to cry.
Try put in so many additives,
so that the food won't spoil.
mark with a sell by date,
and wrap it up in foil.
They load it up with sodium,
and sugar you don't need.
instead of being the lazy one,
you had better start to feed.
Your loved ones with your cooking,
the ones that you adore.
Cook your food at home now,
instead of buying it at the store.

# "MY PILLOW FOR YOU"

While I dream the hours away,
alone in bed at night,
dreaming of the one I love,
and long to hold her tight.

The flashing in my eyes it seems,
my thoughts out of my past,
me together with my love,
I hope that they will last.

I hug my pillow Oh so tight,
and hold it close to me,
I pretend I'm holding her,
her body Oh so free.

As I dream these hours away,
each night to me it's true,
I know that in the future soon,
I'll swap this pillow for you.

# "BE THANKFUL THAT YOU DON'T SMOKE"

Did you ever stop my friend to think,
of all the dirt, the smoke, the stink,
of what your parents said when they spoke,
what would happen if you would smoke.
Do you remember of the way,
you tried to smoke corn silk and hay.
It made you sick from what you did,
but that's all right, your just a kid.
Once a joint you even tried,
and when were asked you even lied.
For you were young and in your prime,
and you'd do anything at that time.
You could do anything in your sight,
if it was wrong, or if it was right.
But you'll find out in later years,
you'll pay then for mothers tears.
Your parents worked hard when you were small,
to keep you always on the ball.
Teach you the way that you would need,
if you were only to succeed.
This little old lady about to crook,
just couldn't make it without her smoke.
The little old guy to stay alive,
carries his oxygen by his side.
They both today would not admit,
if they knew then they would have quit.
But they can't go back there again,
and start their lives without this sin.
So if and when you should look back,
review your footsteps and the track.

The track that brought you up to now,
the parents that worked to show you how.
So say a prayer to up above,
 thank your parents for all their love.
Thank them also for when they spoke,
and also be thankful you didn't smoke.

## "A QUOTE ABOUT LIFE"

Life upon this earth today,
is just a gift you know.
Given from his Grace above,
each day to reap and sow.

Make the best of what you have,
work to make it great.
Do the very best you can,
each day you cultivate.

# "HOW TIME CAN FLY"

Do you remember way back when,
you were young and in your pen?
You played with your toys given to you,
there wasn't much more that you could do.
As time went by day by day,
all you could do is set and play.
Even then you wanted time to fly,
be grown up and say good by.
But then for you it even got worse,
so bad you thought you were in a curse.
Your folks didn't want you to end a fool,
they entered you in grammar school.
Eight years of this didn't fly by,
it dragged along and made you cry.
You really wanted to be free to roam,
all grown up so you could be on your own.
But then it came to your surprise,
and just as sure as the sun will rise.
Off you went to learn the golden rule,
for they entered you in another school.
one was called your high school days,
for you to learn the grown up ways.
Teach you the roads that you must take,
so you'd end up somebody and not a fake.
Time always dragged as days went by,
how you longed for them to fly.
Now that your twentieth year is here,
time has slipped into a higher gear.
You eat and sleep and work all day,
there really isn't anytime to play.

You can't wait for the weekends to come,
so you can go out and have some fun.
As you struggle through life ahead,
the days go by much faster instead.
Your to busy to watch days go by,
and you don't realize how time can fly.

## "BE CONTENT"

Your life could never be so bad,
to make you look and feel so sad.
But when you hate all things in store,
that's when life becomes a bore.

God has picked your life to be,
in a way that you can't see.
But I can say one thing for sure,
life in misery has no cure.

Be content in what you do,
love the life that's given you.
For this life will come and go,
and you'll be old before you know,

So if your miserable as you are,
make a wish upon a star.
For others live much worse than you,
so be content in what you do.

# "A LIFE TIME OF FOUR SCORES"

Just think of what has happened,
in the very last four scores.
In a life that you are living,
you've walked through many doors.

This world has really progressed,
from the beginning to the end.
Within the four scores of our living,
we've come a long way my friend.

We have invented many ways to travel,
with bicycles, autos and trains,
scooters, buses, ships and subways,
along with our fast flying planes.

We can cross this country in hours,
circle the globe in only days.
With all our super highways,
our cars go in many ways.

In a rocket we have invented,
travel all the way to the moon.
Circle the earth for many days,
and come back to be used again soon.

But with all this great knowledge,
and the success that we have shown.
It's a shame that people are greedy,
and keep the profits for their own.

With the shortness of our resources,
and the cost to bring them about,
you would think that some inventors,
could find ways to stretch them out.

Lets take our gas for instance,
a resource that we all use.
In our autos it's a necessity,
some conserve while others abuse.

The cost to purchase a gallon,
back when I was a little boy,
was five gallons for a dollar,
to drive for all of your joy.

An auto in those days would travel,
one hundred miles on this gasoline,
and today it depends on your auto,
about the same distance it would seem.

So where is this inventor?
That invents things for your car.
Can't he invent a carburetor,
that would take us twice as far.

On a gallon of these resources,
that they claim is hard to refine.
cost a dollar fifty a gallon,
to day in our modern time.

Or is it the man in Washington,
or the man that controls the say,
is he the one that is greedy,
in the cost of what we pay.

Or is it this new inventor,
who invented his carburetor so new.
Who was bought off by the oil man,
before it could be brought to you.
I think that it›s a pity,
the rich have all the say.

They control us like some puppets,
and it's us that has to pay.

But that is this modern America,
equal as equal can be.
middleman pays all the taxes,
and the rich ones will always go free.


## "YOUR SURE TO WIN"

As you struggle on through life,
laying out your goals,
adding all the prices up,
and paying all the tolls.

Your hardships may be heavier,
as days they come and go,
but you can bear and face it,
for this I really know.

Hold your head and shoulders high,
and take it on the chin.
Don't give up to anyone,
in the end your sure to win.

# "KEEP OUR FRIENDSHIP TRUE"

The friendship we created,
in our lives when we were young.
things we did together,
the songs that we had sung.

We lived next door to each other,
we played from day to day.
But now that we are older,
its time for me to say.

For now the miles between us,
are more than just a few.
Its hard to get together,
in things we'd love to do.

Our contacts aren't so frequent,
as we both really know,
and trying to make a living,
is one tough row to hoe.

So in the end remember,
I always strive to do.
Keep in contact with my friends,
and keep our friendship true.

# "MY FRONT YARD"

The grass grows tall in my front yard,
it has to be cut each day.
Tie flowers, they bloom to full extent,
the best if I must say.

Tie passers by all stop to look,
to admire all that's in view.
can't believe just what they see,
they don't believe it's true.

They aren't a fake and this I'm sure,
just take it all from me.
I spend half my life in my front yard,
the results is there to see.

You see a yard that's nice and neat,
remember all that I tell.
The owner spends half his life out there,
to make it look that swell.

Sometimes I wonder as life goes by,
if the worth is there in the end.
To have a yard that looks so good,
the payoff for all we spend.

# "MOTHER'S DAY"

We have something dear to us,
that's very close at heart,
and we should work to cherish it,
someday we're going to part.

She brought us two together,
when we were very small,
and if it wasn't for this dear,
we wouldn't be here at all.

She suffered through our making,
she did with best of care,
she struggled through her hardships,
with little time to spare.

For as we all grew older,
her chores grew with us too,
for as our lives went on in time,
she had more work to do.

So think about the payment,
the debt that we all owe,
don't you think that she should harvest,
the crops that she did sow?

Her day again is coming,
when she wakes on this day in May,
don't for get to remember your Mother,
this year on MOTHER'S DAY.

# "HER CHRISTMAS WILL BE WHITE"

I gazed upon a Christmas tree,
back in my home city.
It was on the village green,
and my was it so pretty.

'The lights were shinning all around,
all colors that were bright.
With snow upon the branches too,
to complete that pretty sight.

As I gazed upon this tree,
that kept me hypnotized.
I saw this girl standing there,
and she was sure surprised.

I guess that she had never seen,
a tree like this before.
From birth she had been blinded,
and her sight was just restored.

From this I know the feeling,
a miracle that is right,
and she will be so thankful,
that her Christmas will be white.

# "BE THANKFUL YOUR JOB IS DONE"

I know that you are down and out,
and you think that life's unfair.
But for this very thought my friend,
he knows that you will care.

He put you here into this world,
with a special job to do.
He knows that you will do the job,
and work till you are through.

Some jobs are small and take less time,
if this is in your case.
'Then you should be very pleased my friend,
he trusts that you can face.

He never closes a door on you,
without opening another one.
Be thankful that your job is through,
and think of the upcoming fun.

While others live a longer life,
and suffer all the way.
I know that they would be so glade,
to take your place today.

# "A FISHERMAN'S DREAM"

'The things they had in days gone by,
that lived in fields and streams,
With beauty that could catch your eye,

and fill a sportsman's dreams,
The water bug that lived each day,
to swim and sail his boat,
of all the water things to do,

and more he could promote.
For here it is much later now,
many changes from our past.
Life is in a higher gear,
and we have a brand-new cast.

Seems as though, that some don't care,
what happens in the end
They don't take care of our water today,
and those they should offend.

Now we can't live without it, friend,
no matter how we try.
Unless we work to clean it now,
in the end we're sure to die.

Shall we punish those, who contaminate,
the waters of our streams.
Lets work to rid our pollution today,
and bring back a fisherman's dreams.

I think that it's a pity,
the rich have all the say.
They control us like some puppets,
and it's us that has to pay.
But that is this modern America,
equal as equal can be.
The middle man pays all the taxes,
and the rich ones will always go free.

# "LIFE UPON THIS EARTH EACH DAY"

Life upon this earth each day,
is just a gift you know.
Given by his grace above,
each day to reap and sow.

Make the best of what you have,
work to make it great.
Thank the lord in some small way,
each day you cultivate.

Don't stress upon your aches and pains,
you'll find it's really sad.
For there are others that you know,
that have it twice as bad.

# "A SPECIAL DAY"

A special day comes once a year,
and when it does your older.
So when this day comes for my wife,
I love to kiss and hold her.

This we've done for many years,
for she is thirty-seven,
and if and when you talk to her,
she'd say that she's from heaven.

But I love her just the same,
her age it means no more.
Two people living just as one,
in a lifetime of four score.

For here we are in a lifetime dear,
your age it never grows,
No matter dear how old you are,
your beauty is what shows.

So have a happy Birthday,
the best one in your life,
and I'll be so happy dear,
for me you are my wife.

# "A LIFE ALONE"

When I was just a little boy,
about the age of three.
The good lord saw it fittingly,
to take my mom from me.

He knew that I could get along,
without her tender love.
He took her far away from me,
to somewhere up above.

Now I was doing nicely,
under my father's care,
The good lord began to figure,
once again that I could spare.

So he chose to take my father,
the love of my dear dad.
He left me once again alone,
to make good or to turn bad.

Now that I'm much older,
and look at days gone by,
to remember of my childhood,
each time it makes me cry.

I wonder how it might have been,
if my parents could be with me,
and live a life as normal kids,
Since that day that I turned three.


I know that life's a struggle,
each day that it was sad.
This story has been a true one,
because I was that lad.

# "OUR LIVES WILL NEVER BE THE SAME"

As one lives theirs lives each day,
from in the past to make life pay,
they choose what is best always for them,
to make their lives a real great gem.

The good from the bad, they separate,
to create a life, to them that is great.
The sadness, the sorrow, they put aside,
To build happiness and Joy, to lift their pride.

But when you are hit with a tourist attack,
like on 9-11, you can't turn your back,
You must show your loyalty, like the rest,
and work to survive, all hardships the best.

Restore life, overcome problems at hand,
Work to build security within our land.
Eliminate terrorism, send them al] home,
Don't let them within, our country to roam.

But really for us to overcome the sorrow,
it will never be the same for us tomorrow,
We'll do our best to survive all at stake,
To rebuild our lives and overcome this quake

# "THE GREETINGS OF RACY DAY"

As one wakes each morning,
to greet a brand-new day.
Be thankful to the Lord above,
and do it in your own way,

Take a moment to consider,
what is there ahead of you.
and plan the program of the day,
in the work that you must do,

Enjoy all those around you,
and the weather as it may be.
If the weather is not to your liking,
it will change, just wait and see.

In the winter it is unpleasant,
always cold, with nothing in bloom.
But we put up with what were given,
and pray that spring will come soon.

The traveling to the workplace,
is a necessity that you can't avoid.
Keep an eye on those around you,
you don't want your day destroyed.

In the spring and summer it is better,
on days when you are free.
To vacation somewhere in our country,
and learn of the beauty we see.

So when you awake each morning,
'ay Your prayer to his lord above,
and be thankful your health is outstanding,
and your able to live the life that you love.

# "BEE'S GALORE"

A hive, a honey bee calls home,
perched on it's base with a dome,
most usually it is painted white,
so each little bee can see in flight.

Once this little bee enters the door,
there are bee's everywhere, galore,
each one working in his own way,
as each one does, day after day.

Expert pilots, while in flight,
collecting honey from morning till night.
Storing the honey within the cone,
each one working without a moan.

When the summer comes to an end,
this the message that they all send.
Work each day, do your very best,
leave the worrying to the rest.

There will be plenty of food for you,
if you do what you are suppose to do,
throughout the winter and days ahead,
you can lie comfortably within your bed.

# "THE LOVERS OF DEVILED EGGS"

The eggs were selected at random,
each weighed for a perfect fit,
then placed in a pan for boiling,
seemed a time that would never quit

Removed from the heat after completion,
placed in cold water to cool them down.
It's time to dissect them from their covers,
placed in halves so perfectly round.

The yolks, we place in a bowl,
a filling we are about to make,
we add the spices for the flavor,
special care is what we take.

Placed in the holes of their bodies,
lined up on a platter so neat.
So delicious to even look at,
you can't wait for your chance to eat.

You've eaten these at other meetings,
and enjoyed them every time.
But today under different condition,
will the taste be up to your prime,

We hope you enjoy when your eating,
these eggs as they are put in your view,
the maker whom you'll never know,
did the best that anyone could do.

So enjoy them during their existence,
right down to the very last one,
and remember to thank the maker,
for a job that is always well done.

# "A PRAYER FOR DAD"

Even though we're left behind,
with Dad's thoughts and love.
We know he's in a special care,
by his Grace above.

We miss Dad more as hours go by,
and say our prayers each day.
Our thoughts will always be with him,
within our work and play.

# "A VETERAN'S THOUGHTS"

A story about veterans should be told
either their young, middle aged or old.
many a request that comes to me,
js help the veterans, in their troubles we see,

Yes, this is something that's true as gold,
and lets work together as we unfold.
A program formatted to help them out,
and make them strong again and stout.

They gave their time, when they were asked,
out of their lives somewhere in their past.
To help their country, in time of war,
Let's help them now to settle the score.

Now it's our Country's job, to cover the past,
of those veterans today in need they ask.
No matter if it's health, food, or other needs
the federal government should cover these deeds

'Those candidates we put in office you'll find,
only care about themselves, in this hardship time.
They cover their tracks down each ones road,
80 their retiring days, won't have a hardship load.

You don't stop to think, when you ask me to give,
that I might be one also in the life I live,
Don't ask a veteran in these times to give more,
It's your Uncle Sam's Job to settle the score.


As veterans we should work together as a team,
come up with a Program that's full of steam.
Work on a Project to change some of our laws,
to cover the mishaps, from the words from our jaws.

# "BEAUTY FOR YOU TO ADORE"

High in the mountains
Up there in the breeze,
Doing what comes natural,
Just as we all please.

The beauty when you see it,
That takes your breath away.
It is my kind of living,
And usually makes your day.

While there, you have no worry,
Your free as free can be.
Enjoying the things around you,
Viewing all there is to see.

So if you get the chance,
While opportunity knocks at your door,
Take off to the mountains,
And see the beauty there to adore.

# "SNOW GALORE"

As the snow fell to the ground,
And the wind blew it around,
Piled it up in mounds so deep,
Hard to walk or even creep.

A beautiful sight for you to see,
And even you will have to agree.
All the children will love to play,
in this stuff both night and day.

Skiers too will fill their joy,
As snow mobiles become the toy.
Slide the little ones down the hill,
Be sure their safe and they don't spill.

This white stuff that we all so love,
fell to earth from his Grace above.
God's gift to us, the young and the old,
It's part of life as I am told.

But those of us on this Precious day,
must remove this stuff that's in our way.
Driveway and sidewalks, free of the snow,
So you will be safe wherever you go.

In days ahead the temperature will rise,
the snow will be gone to your surprise,
It melts to water and flows away,
to make even more of a perfect day,

So enjoy the Snow while it is around,
Enjoy it's beauty while on the ground,
After a while it becomes a bore,
known to us as "SNOW GALORE"

In memory of all those that were lost in the trage-
dy at the Station nightclub, in West Warwick, RI.

Written by Jerry Moothart in their behalf.

# "NOT GOOD-BY, BUT JUST SO LONG"

They've gone from here on earth today,
and this is sad we know,
For all their friends and loved ones, left,
each day to reap and sow.

But their memories will remain with us,
throughout the days to come.
Of their past lives, with family and friends,
that made them that special someone.

Take care in heaven and rest in peace,
our thoughts are there with you,
for it's a tragedy that you were in,
there was nothing that you could do.

Your family and friends will continue on,
down the walks here left behind,
and keep the thoughts of each of you,
that were so sweet and kind.

Things happen in our lives each day,
that we cannot explain,
For God has Picked to end your lives,
in this way and it's a shame a shame.

For here on earth in the records it reads,
your gone to a life of heaven and song.
For us left here on earth, we would like to say,
not good-by, but just so long.

# "CHRISTMAS COMES BUT ONCE A YEAR"

CHRISTMAS comes but once a year,
the time for us that is so dear.
A birthday remembrance for Christ we know,
would be so great without the snow,

When we were young and in our prime,
the snow back then we didn't mind.
To skate on ice and ski on snow,
was really great oh don't you know.

Now that we are in our upper years,
snow and ice is in our fears.
It would be better within our care,
if that cold weather was never there.

Although we know there is places I'm sure,
with a temperature great to fit a cure.
So when your blood it slows it's pace,
your able to survive in the daily race.

You planted your roots, in a place it's true,
a place you love and is dear to you.
You can't just up and move away,
because cold weather it comes your way.

So take the HOLIDAYS your about to review.
may they be the best this year for you.
For on these days take special cares,
we'll keep you in our daily prayers.

# "MOTHER SPIDER"

A mother spider from her web,
instructed her children as she said,
this web to you, it may look crude,
I spun it here to catch our food.

You, too must learn as you all grow,
in days ahead so you will know,
just how to weave one in and out,
to really make it strong and stout.

Yes back and forth, and up and down,
go many times round and round,
so in your mind when you are through,
you'll know that it will work for you.

When you are satisfied that it's your best,
then it will be time for you to rest,
to set back within your home and nap,
to wait for a creature to enter your trap.

When it does then you will know,
it's time for you to be on the go,
take care of the creature in your own way,
so you'll have food for a rainy day.

To feed the little ones, to make them grow,
while in your heart you'll always know.
that in your life you did the test,
you raised your children your very best,

So down the road in life beyond,
as Mother Spider, you will be fond,
in your heart, you'll always know,
you taught them well, the rows to hoe.

# "FORGE'S AT PLAY"

A mother frog throughout the day,
continues to watch her young at play,
from her Lilly pad up so high,
watches the little ones as they go by.

As they swim by to and fro,
diving and leaping as they go,
she sets there many hours of her day,
teaching each one within their play.

Where to hide from creatures ahead,
listen to others don't get mislead,
be on guard all hours of the day,
especially while your in your play.

Then when it's time to leave your home,
enter the world as you roam,
think of the lessons your mother taught,
and into trouble don't get caught.

As you set on your Lilly pad high,
watch your children as they go by,
and teach them what was taught to you,
a life that is so straight and true.

# "THANKSGIVING DAY"

Our heavenly Father, as we all gather,
upon this special day.
We all join hands, and open our hearts.
together as we all say.

Our thanks to you, the creator of all,
for the blessings that you have bestowed.
Upon each and every one of us,
and our thanks to you that is owed.

We're especially thankful for our lives,
and this day so we may gather.
To set around this beautiful table,
and for the food that is on each platter.

Yes to you Lord, from one and all,
of us together as we say.
THANK YOU LORD, THANK YOUR LORD,
On this beautiful Thanksgiving Day.

# "SHARING OUR JOYS WITH THE NEEDY"

There are many, many children,
within this world today.
were brought into their environment,
and didn't even have a say.

By an enjoyment of their parents,
some planned and some were not.
While some were taken care of,
but many, many were forgot.

To us that are more fortunate,
and are well off in our lives today.
Should consider some kind of enjoyment,
within our work and in our play.

To think about those little ones,
many out there all alone.
Who have no one to love them,
and many without a home.

If we would just consider,
all the enjoyment that we would get.
If we thought about those little ones,
in the past that we just met.

To bring about some happiness,
a joy within your reason.
while filling the needs of some little ones,
during the days of this Christmas season.

# "THOSE GOOD OLD NAVY DAYS"

When I first hit the Worcester,
back in the fall of 49.
It was a great experience to living,
for this young guy at that time.

But in the days that followed,
it was fun and days of joy.
for this fresh kid out of high school,
ambitious and a growing boy.

Yes in the days that followed,
the ship was on the go.
To places, you never heard of,
but places you'd like to know.

I had a great time cruising,
those four years that were new.
To think back it brings memories,
as a member of that crew.

I met a lot of friends there,
and many were on the ball.
this sailor they called HOOT,
is one I don't recall.

But if I had more information,
as to where, how and when,
this sailor served his country,
aboard the Worcester, yes my friend.

I was in the E division,
those days I served with pride.
But where did HOOT hang out,

where on that ship did he hide.
We served our country with honors,
in the Korean conflict as it was named.
Took the United Nations only three years,
for this conflict to be tamed.

Shortly after then I left her,
the Worcester far behind,
to look for other interest,
somewhere in this world to find.

I ended up in Boston,
a city far from home.
and it's here I sunk my anchor,
no more this world to roam.

I tried to keep up with the Worcester,
in the days that were ahead,
I searched for all kinds of material,
from all the things I read.

I met a few of the sailors,
in the days once on the shore.
They gave me no information,
of the Worcester so I could score.

As to its where about and ventures,
or to its final resting place.
But I found out they had junked it,
and this I had to face.

In all the miles I traveled,
those four years way back then.
Four trips to the Mediterranean,
with it's knowledge we apprehend.

All the trips to the Caribbean,
and that trip around the world.
Through both of the large canals,
would cause you hair to curl.
Our stay in Pearl Harbor,
Venice, Trieste, and many more.
Colombo, Gibraltar, the Riviera,
on the list of these galore.

While here I end my reminiscing,
the fun we had in many ways.
All the days that were spent there,
in "THOSE GOOD OLD NAVY DAYS".

# "A LITTLE BOY AT CHRISTMAS."

As a little boy I was unhappy,
as unhappy as can be.
For there I stood just looking,
beneath the Christmas tree.

For what I asked from Santa,
I could not really believe.
That Santa could have forgotten,
to stop on Christmas eve.

I guess this is what happens,
when you break the rules your told,
and you sneak to spy on Santa,
who does his job so bold.

I creep back to my bedroom,
I crawl back into bed,
and I thought about my wishes,
and what my mother said.

I couldn't return to sleeping,
my wish was on my mind,
and I thought for sure dear Santa,
would come and be so kind.

My mother called next morning,
come down, she said to me,
and there my wish was granted,
beneath the Christmas tree.

My thanks goes out to Santa,
for he in his generous way,
has made this a beautiful
Christmas,
I'll remember till my dying day.

# "ALZHEIMER'S"
## A KILLER IS ON THE LOOSE

ONE OF OUR REASONS OF BEING HERE TODAY.
IS TO SUPPORT OUR CHARITY IN EVERY WAY.
WE ASK OF YOU TO JOIN WITH US.
AS WE DO OUR BEST TO CATCH THIS CUSS.

HE'S OUT THERE ROAMING, FREE TO KILL.
WE MUST REMOVE HIM OF THIS FREE WILL.
SAVE OUR FAMILIES, OUR FRIENDS, OURSELVES,
FROM THIS KILLER AS HISTORY TELLS.

DO YOUR BEST IN WHAT YOU GIVE,
IN HONOR OF THOSE THAT STILL LIVE,
AND ALL OF THOSE HE KILLED BEFORE,
YOU MIGHT BE NEXT HE'S LOOKING FOR.

BY GIVING TODAY IS A TWO TIME PLEASURE,
ONE THAT YOU WILL ALWAYS TREASURE.
SO GIVE WHATEVER YOU CAN SPARE,
TO FIND A CURE AND HELP WITH CARE.

WE THANK YOU IN ADVANCE FOR YOUR SUPPORT,
TO HELP US TODAY SO WE CAN ABORT.
TO STOP THIS PAIN AND ALL THIS ABUSE,
AND CATCH THIS KILLER THAT'S ON THE LOOSE.

# "MONEY FOR MY FUTURE"

In the beginning of my life,
When I was very small,
I was just a chubby guy,
I was not very tall.

In my travels off to school
One day to my surprise.
A penny came within my view,
There just before my eyes.

This is my lucky piece
I thought there to myself.
For it could be the foundation,
It's the beginning of my wealth.

If I should invest it wisely,
And I could make it grow.
It could make me a million,
In the future don't you know?

Now that I'm much older,
And retirement is in view.
Today I have the knowledge,
I know what I should do.

But back there in my childhood,
With my thoughts there as a kid,
It will only take a moment,
To tell you what I did.

I did the same as all kids.
What they do when they are small.
They don't think of the future,

For most don't care at all.
It's easy come to them my friend,
And just as fast will go,
While nothing will be put away,
To see if will grow.

So the government should tax you,
For your retirement and old age,
For when you reach the retirement time,
You can draw from this your wage.

This would be your money,
Like a savings account for you,
So after your retirement,
You can live a life and do.

The things you've always longed for,
And see the places you've never seen,
And pay for all the enjoyment,
That makes a retirement keen.

You say we already have this,
 Social Security is its name.
But really when you look at it,
The two are not the same,

For here is Social Security,
You help to fill the pot,
And this is raised for everyone,
Those working and those that did not.

The figure that you draw each month,
Is standard to us all,
Governed by the length of time,
You were ambitious and on the ball.

So if you should expire,
And your life comes to an end,
That pay you draw from S.S.,
S.S. will no longer send.
The rest that you contributed,
Is gone from your account,
The debt that they owe you,
Is zero to any amount?

So why can't it be deposited,
Into a file listing your name,
To grow until your sixty-five,
Retirement coming from the same.

Upon death all that remains there,
Becomes part of your estate,
Be divided among your survivors,
Those listed there on that date.

I'm now working for my retirement,
Those days way down the trail,
To have enough money established,
So my retirement days won't fail.

You too should make this available,
Establish a 401K banking account,
As you work for your retirement.
Each week depositing a certain amount.

# "FROM STINKY POO TO CHUBBY CHEEKS"

Your Pa Pa called you stinky Poo,
when you were very small,
and it was very appropriate,
for one who couldn't crawl.

But when you stopped to think of it,
the name it wasn't true.
For Pa Pa's little sweetheart,
that name would never do.

So Pa Pa picked a truer name,
a name that's true to shine.
Now Chubby Cheeks is what he calls,
his Grandson every time.

A bundle of smiles, a face that's shines,
with cheeks that puff with joy.
A treasure in a Mother's heart,
her precious little boy.

He never cries, he never pouts,
His wants are very small,
if it wasn't for his coos and sighs,
you wouldn't know he's there at all.

Yes this little joy at heart,
is true in every way.
He's Pa Pa's little Chubby Cheeks,
and he makes his Pa Pa's day.

# "PUTTING ON THAT SMILE"

Each life we are given at time of birth,
is a gift from God above.
We should cherish this gift so true,
by repaying him with our love.

As we enter our lives each day,
with a smile upon our face,
for this will keep us fit and trim,
a feeling that's hard to replace.

Sometimes we look in work or play,
at shadows on a face not clowning,
and if you checked I'm sure you'd find,
a face that's frequently frowning.

Light represents the joyfulness,
while looking at yourself in the mirror,
of what you see and how you look,
to those so close and dear.

A gray reflection of sadness it's true,
like a cloud that hides the sun,
the radiance of joy and happiness gone,
in a life without any fun.

To see the colors around ourselves,
in the laughter of each mankind,
the children, the adults look for glow,
in the happiness of friends they find.

Let's emphasize on things of good,
not dwell on what's done to us,
while we keep a positive look on life,

and live to cause no fuss.
Those flowers that are growing free,
while in shadows they sometimes grow,
but always stretching towards the sun,
while others will die you know.

Nothing exists within a gloom,
eventually all things will die,
for we can't live beyond our time,
no matter how hard we try.

Sometimes we find we're down and out,
and we must work it's true,
perseverance and courage we must regain,
towards the goals that we renew.

Now all the while throughout our lives,
let's pause for just a while,
and try to look our very best,
by putting on that smile.

## "THE ONES WE LOVE"

Our heavenly father from up above,
look down and protect the ones we love.
Take special care we ask today,
of our little ones while in their play.
Protect this nursery with your touch,
the little ones here we love so much.
For if it is within your grace,
make each day special for them to face.
And, when in time this day is through,
in their own way they'll say thanks to you.

AMEN

# "A GRANDSON SO TRUE"

Do you know Justin from Mansfield Town?
so sweet to meet and be around.
has a sister and she's sweet too,
both of them so kind and true.
He travels a lot to school each day,
then to the Y where he can play.
At home with a Gameboy called SP,
likes to play golf but has no tee.
Walks with papa on the streets to store,
and picks up cans that are galore.
Found a golf ball while doing this trick,
jumped the guardrail to get it quick.
Crossed two bridges at the golf course true,
something he always wanted to do.
He wanted to walk to the graveyard where,
great, great grandma and daughter are there.
His father suddenly drove down the street,
offered to remove him from his feet.
To ride in the truck the rest of the way home,
get ready for bed; put an end to his roam.
That's how it is as a sweet little boy,
a gem to his Papa, his precious living toy.
Justin works in the garden, swims in the pool,
working real hard to learn the golden rule.
Listens to the grown--ups, does what he's told to do,
known to his Papa, as "A GRANDSON SO TRUE".

# "AS THE SOUTHPAW SHE IS"

My daughter blessed me with a child,
awesome, cute and sometimes wild.
After a few years had gone by,
something outstanding caught our eye.

As her Papa, it was great to see,
this little girl looked just like me.
With straight hair, hanging low,
sometimes braided, or in a bow.

Katrina McIntosh is her name,
rides her bike and scooter with fame.
Plays in the back yard with her toys
Swims in the pool to fill her joys

She started to write she took her stand,
We noticed the pen in her left hand,
and this is why from what I saw,
that I nicked named her my, South Paw.

Now kindergarten, first year of school,
she's there to learn the golden rule.
The ins and outs, the ups and down,
all right here in our Mansfield town.

She reads her books and plays her game,
gets unruly and she is hard to tame.
Papa loves her, endure what he saw,
that is why I call her my South Paw.

# "COPIED A BIRD AND GAVE US A PLANE"

Many, many years ago,
when God put men on this earth,
he also gave them other things,
to make life here what it's worth.

Most of the things were enjoyable,
while others were not so sweet,
all those pesky mosquitoes,
that suck blood from your arms and feet.

As man observed the surroundings,
all the things there in their view,
one of the objects that impressed them,
is birds and what they do.

Those beautiful flying fowls,
all sizes, with their actions in the sky,
they thought that it would be so nice,
if they too could also fly.

Along came the Wright Brothers,
their thoughts brought into hand,
they put together the necessary things,
to get man off of this land.

At the very first it was a scary thing,
and slowly each day as it grew,
It improved and got much better,
each time the Wright Brothers flew.

Now if you look at flying today,
it's still a challenge at hand,
each time a plane at take off,

and comes back again to land.
Some airports, they are too small,
and the noise it's out of control,
for those that live nearby,
is very aggravating to their soul.

But the usefulness of the airplane,
is a must within life each day,
as you climbed aboard for takeoff,
and it gets you on your way.

Now think of all the progress,
the difference now than from our past,
 that was copied from a flying bird,
and the trails that birds all cast.

The birds are all left behind,
as planes fly faster and higher each to go,
smaller planes even fly upside down,
birds can't do this, as you know.

They fly over the world each day,
even some on a special trip,
and several have landed on the noon,
even birds couldn't make this flip.

Let's all be very thankful,
God formatted life so we can't complain,
He gave some all the knowledge,
to copy a bird and gave us a plane.

# "CHANGES NEED TO BE MADE"

They gave their lives for their country.
Buried in the tomb of the unknown where they lay.
They watched over the destiny of our country.
Seen all changes made from day to day.

As I look back at what I fought for.
Our flag the red, white and blue.
The loyalty to those left at home.
In our country that is so true.

When I was called to fight for my country,
It was a duty that everyone did.
To protect our country and our future,
We were taught in our schooling as a kid.

While some gave more than the others,
To us it was really not fair.
To give their lives for our country,
And fight for those who don't care

Today is the payoff of that fighting?
The offspring of those that came home,
All others allowed in this country.
All free to live here and to roam.

While honoring the things that we stand for,
The loyalty to a country one should give.
To respect the colors of Old Glory.
Supporting this country where you live.

But many refused to agree to this.
They won't work for what they receive.
They expect to be handed daily.
Payment for the nothings they achieve.
While some love it on welfare.
Unemployment is the way they are paid.

Every day to them is a vacation.
And for those they really have it made.

Its here we have to make changes.
The immigrants allowed coming here.
Too many are entering our country.
Not legally throughout each year.

We have to cut back on our imports.
Return to what's called "American Made".
Create jobs for the American people.
While watching as unemployment will fade.

Tax our people so all are equal.
Not the way that it is of late.
For those that live by a border.
Do shopping in a much cheaper state.

For those that work for the government.
Today these workers don't care.
They all make enough money.
They can afford to pay any fare.

The tax laws are created for them.
The loopholes they all can crawl through.
It's the workers in much lower brackets.
They pay dearly like me and yes you.

So let's all pool our forces together.
Work to create all the changes today.
That's needed to rebuild our country.
Create laws so we equally all pay.

Elect those that will work in high office.
Rewriting laws needed for the change.
Not just those that are looking for glory.
Put our country back on a growing range.
Start by securing all the borders.
Both north and south close the door.

Start removing all of the illegal immigrants.
That sneaked into our country before.

Work to make changes in our manufacturing
So the production will resume on our land.
Change laws increasing the import and export taxation.
That will release the burden on those here at hand.

Social security should be equal to everyone.
All paying into and receiving the same.
Not the programs as they are instituted
Some get much more and this is a shame.

Our medical programs all need to be worked on.
All insurance and medications those are too high.
The manufacturers are making a very large profit.
Yes and for this, we all should know why.

Oils another item listed that needs our attention.
Change the cost to produce and where it comes from.
If the officers of our country are the owners,
Then this job I'm sure will never get done.

It was God who created our country.
He watched over while the foundation was laid,
 God We Trust should remain in our history.
Taught in our schools this rule should not fade.

The English language is there in our foundation.
All living here should be mandate for its use
Other languages are not needed in our country.
To use them here in this country is an abuse.

You learn more in this country while observing.
You know as I what we need to survive.
So lets all unite together throughout the process,
And work to keep America alive.

# "IT'S NOT MY JOB"

It's not my job to be the boss,
employees I can't hire,
and if the ones you have don't work,
It's not my place to fire.

I cannot purchase nor receive,
nor can I attempt to sell,
but if this business goes in the red,
just see who catches hell.

# "PLEASE NOTE"

The next five poems were written for the promotional Purpose of The improved Order of Red Men and the Degree of Pocahontas. This Fraternal Order for both the Sisters and Brothers as members was one of the oldest American originated fraternal Orders which dated back to the colonial days where the members then fought for our freedom we share today. As a thirty-year member of both Orders and holding a title of Past Great Incohonee, (Past National President), Brother Moothart wrote these poems to use on programs to promote the Order.

# "FREEDOM, FRIENDSHIP AND CHARITY"

The Improved Order of Red Men,
With its Sisters, the D. of P.
One of the oldest American Fraternities,
Is out there for all to see.

The precepts of our beloved order,
We work with from day to day.
Are always available for our members,
In our work, and in our play.

Freedom is what we worked for,
Many years back in our past,
And today we keep right on working,
To make sure that it will last.

Next here comes the Friendship,
In our order this must be true.
It has to be there for our members,
Yes him, and her and you.

Now Charity is the best one,
The labors for us are twofold.
To work hard for those in needy,
Is a pleasure as I am told.

So let's spread the history of our order,
There are many that don't even know.
The more we advertise our fraternity,
Is the only way that we can grow.

Also work to improve our precepts,
Built as well as they can be.
A sound foundation for our order,
Known to us as F, F, and C.

# "THIS COIN WITHIN MY HAND"

I have a coin within my hand,
and it's not hard to understand.
A silver dollar comparable in size,
what it represents is no surprise.
One hundred fifty years of our past,
a history with a marvelous cast.
The Great Council of the United States,
 to this part of our history is where it relates.
Our name is there for all to see,
the Eagle flies as free as can be,
and on the back, yes to your surprise,
what's written there for all our eyes.
FREEDOM, in languages in thirteen ways,
for thirteen countries to really prays.
The thirteen ways, blind people without fail,
for them it's written, there in Braille.
What this coin will do, for you,
will do its part for you it's true.
When laid out flat upon its back,
will spin so true within its track
Then when it stops from its long spin,
will tell the one that did not win.
So if the arrow should point to you,
it's your fair job for you to do.
Yes, you must up and fatten the till,
for your responsible to pay the bill.

# "A TOTAL OF ALL FUNDS"

Picking up cans along the streets and road,
on certain occasions becomes a heavy load.
Who cares about the weight if you're having fun,
and the benefits of the efforts goes to everyone.

If the deposits on the cans is put to good taste,
all your time while doing so won't go to waste.
So pick some time in your life and put it aside,
the outcome for doing so you won't have to hide.

Collect cans along with those used at home,
and in all your travels when you have to roam,
Then cash them in at the center for refund,
this payment for efforts in all you have done.

Then donate the total to our National Charity,
to increase the amount for you and for me.
So in days ahead, we hope they will find,
a cure for ALZHEIMER'S in some way of some kind.

"ALZHEIMER'S" kills thousands each day of each year,
and we all would love to live without fear.
So let's all work harder, coral this killer on the loose,
and put a stop to that pain, and all this abuse.

Can I count on you, to add your name on our list,
to help this committee in their efforts to assist.
To build the donations to our charity in the next two great suns.
1500 we would like, for "A TOTAL OF ALL FUNDS.

# "AN APPLICATION"

An application, is here given to you,
only you with it know what to do.
Find that one member, for our Fraternity,
new ones we're always, happy to see.

Go out of your way to find someone,
eager to help and have some fun.
There are many out there we'd love to know,
as members, would help our Fraternity grow.

A dedicated member as you say, you are,
 sign up a candidate and become a star.
Be a sponsor of the one, that you bring in,
so our organization will be the one to win.

# "THE REBUILDER'S OF OUR FUTURE"

As we observe the future,
and the history of our past.
We have to make some changes,
if we expect to last.

We must gear ourselves in society,
modern times of living today.
Put together a brand-new picture,
if we expect to stay.

We're no longer a secret society,
and no longer do we have to hide.
Let's plan a big course of advertising,
and put all other thoughts aside.

To operate our beloved order,
yes, to improve it once again.
To make it more appealing,
so all of our members will win.

So we can do much better,
with sociability in our trend.
That in our immediate future,
our order will be on the mend.

To also upgrade our precepts,
so that we can do much more,
to build within our fraternity,
a bond greater than before.

To do this will take the membership,
yes each and everyone.
Working together in unity,
yes working and having fun.

I've pledge to work as a leader,
to give it my total all.
I hope that you will be counted,
as one to be there on the ball.

Let's not wait any longer,
the time to begin is now.
Join those that are your leaders,
if you need someone to show you how.

For those of us in the future,
that work together as we send,
a message to all the members,
that our Order is on the mend.

We ask for you to join us,
for your help we hope and pray,
Join the reconstructions of our Order
as we work hard, day, by day.

www.ingramcontent.com/pod-product-compliance
Lightning Source LLC
Chambersburg PA
CBHW020324130626
46549CB00003B/1004